SHIP

David Macaulay

Houghton Mifflin Company   Boston   1993

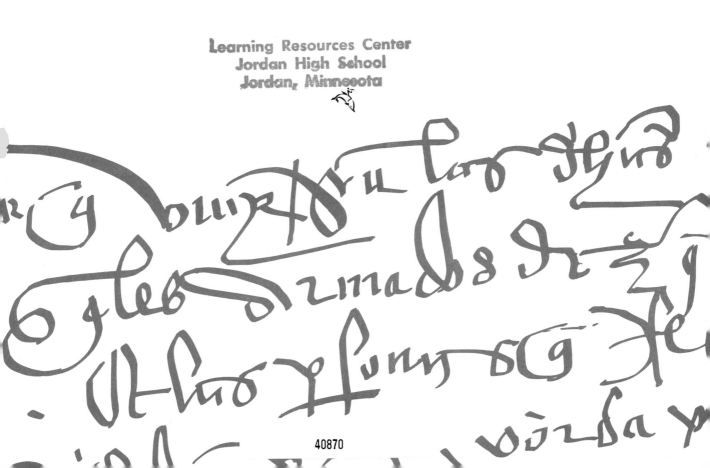

for
Heather Lynne Coppola
and
Thomas Hancock Joslin

Maria Sousa is beginning to feel the strain. She has spent four hours at the end of a tow line looking straight down. Eight meters below, her shadow glides effortlessly over the sea bed. A diver's tip has lured Sousa and her fellow maritime archaeologists to the Brazos del Diablo reef in search of an anchor and whatever other clues might remain of an early-sixteenth-century wreck—possibly a caravel.

Suddenly she releases the line and hovers above the encrusted anchor, its form barely visible against the sandy bottom. After alerting the boat, she and her partner, Jack Stevens, strap on diving equipment and go down for a closer look. The rock-hard coating that engulfs the anchor also cements it to the ocean floor. Less than five meters away, several encrusted swivel guns are similarly glued in place. Neither the anchor nor the guns appear to have moved in a very long time.

A trail of ballast stones and lead shot steers the pair toward the top of the reef, beyond which stretches a white sandy plain dotted with elkhorn coral, gorgonia, and sea fans. While most of the vegetation grows at random, the gorgonia is an exception. It rises from the furrowed sea bed in two distinct rows. Gently brushing the sand from around the base of one stem at a time, Sousa and Stevens discover that beneath each gorgonia sprig is the top of a squared timber. And on the dark and saturated surfaces of each timber are the unmistakable marks of the carpenter's blade that originally shaped them.

A sudden clanging signals them to the surface, where fellow archaeologist Alan Keiffer and Cherubian government representative Felix Morp point anxiously toward a bank of dark clouds. As the team retreats to the safety of the mother ship, Sousa and Stevens excitedly describe what they have uncovered. But by the time the storm passes, so too has the light.

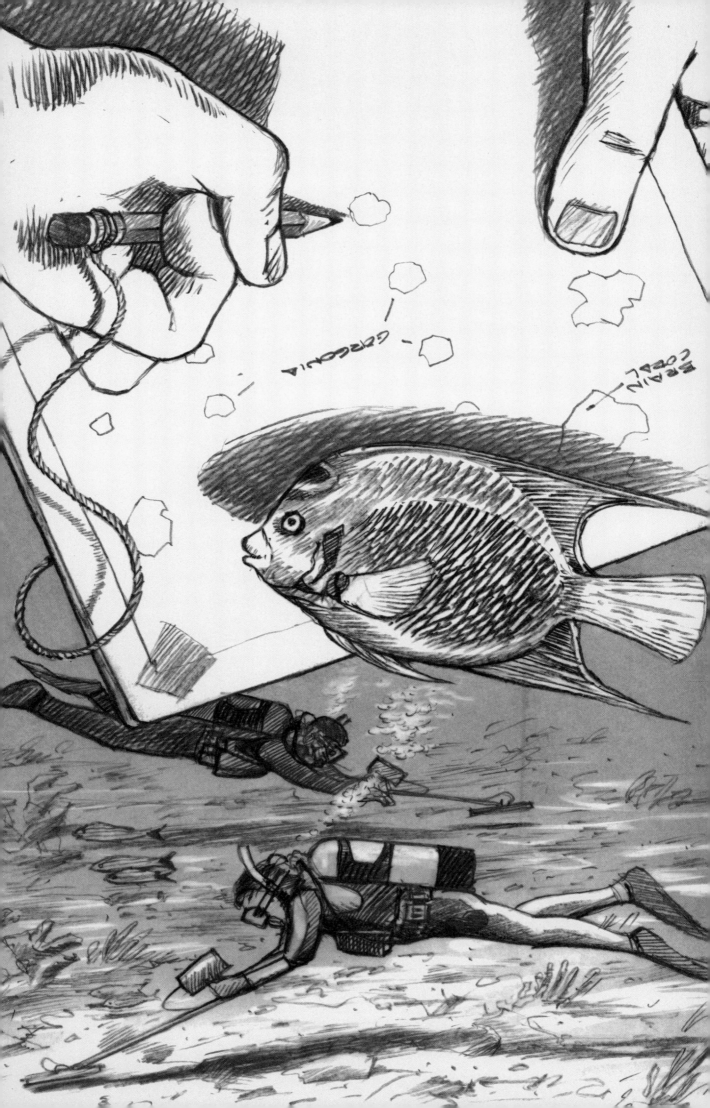

Taking advantage of clear skies and a calm sea, the team is back on the site early the following morning. Working almost without interruption until seven o'clock that evening, Sousa and Morp photograph the area, while Stevens and Keiffer draw an accurate plan.

On the third day, they begin to explore things that cannot yet be seen. Working near the rows of gorgonia, Stevens inserts a steel rod straight down into the sand until it will go no farther. Keiffer then notes the depth of the probe. After the two men repeat this process at regular intervals, the numbers begin to define an otherwise invisible mound of stones—ballast once stored below deck to keep a sailing ship upright in strong winds. To add to the picture, Sousa and Morp use metal detectors in their search for other objects hidden below the surface of the sand.

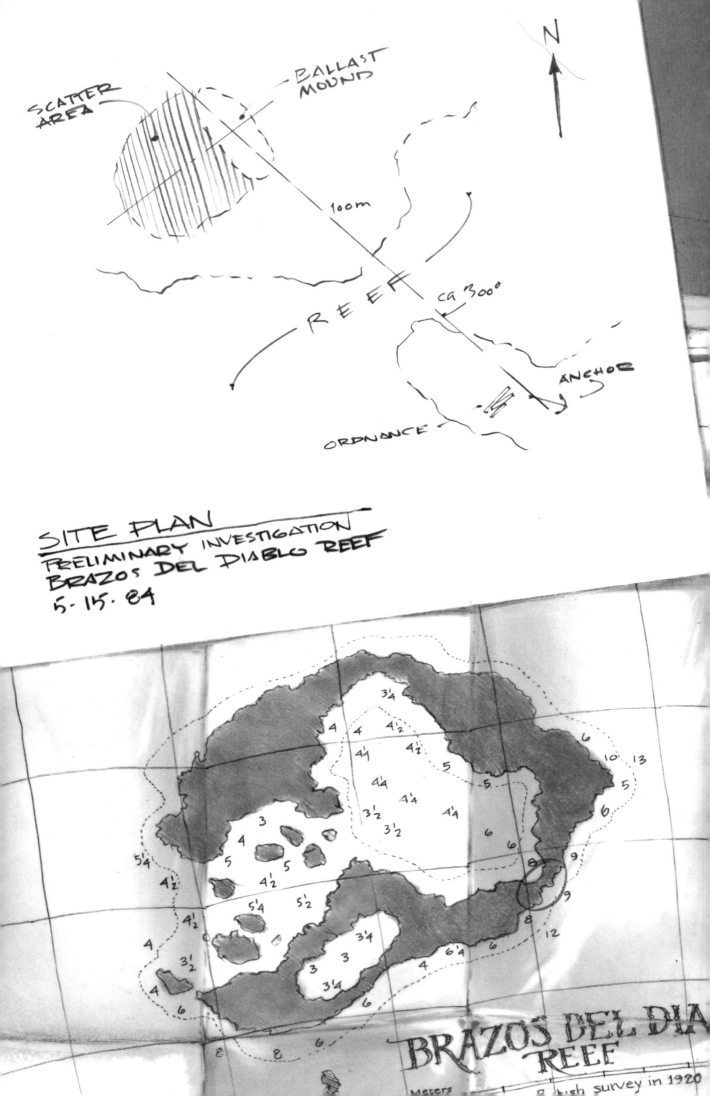

SCATTER AREA

BALLAST MOUND

N

100m

REEF

ca 300°

ANCHOR

ORDNANCE

SITE PLAN
PRELIMINARY INVESTIGATION
BRAZOS DEL DIABLO REEF
5·15·84

BRAZOS DEL DIA
REEF

tish survey in 1920

Meters

RIDA

B A H A M A S

N

C U B A

8000

All four archaeologists are optimistic that this is indeed the final resting place of a very old ship. Although brief, the survey has identified three distinct areas of the site. The first is the path of artifacts from the outer bank to the top of the reef. The second is the location of the remains of a vessel as defined by traces of timber and ballast. The third area, called the scatter site, contains isolated metal objects that most likely spilled from the ship as it sank.

It is eight o'clock in the evening before the exhausted crew sits down to dinner. At sunrise, they will be on their way to another site in the Bahamas where the rest of the team is already at work on a late-sixteenth-century wreck.

By September, the members of Maritime Archaeological Research are back on firm ground. Kansas, in fact. A chain lift, which once hoisted worn-out engines from pickup trucks, slowly lowers a five-hundred-year-old cannon into a vat of preservative solution. Similar tanks cover most of the oil-stained concrete floor, and storage cabinets and shelves line the walls. Most excavations produce a wealth of objects, all of which require proper housing before, during, and after they are studied. Anticipating the retrieval of an overwhelming number of new artifacts, the archaeologists were forced to move off the Overland University campus and into a pair of vacant garage buildings.

In mid-November, Stevens finally completes his report on the Brazos survey for the Cherubian government. In it he offers three reasons why the site deserves excavation. First, there is good reason to believe that a sizable portion of a wooden hull may still be intact below the ballast mound. Second, the large number of possible artifacts located by the metal detectors suggests that the site was not salvaged when the ship went down. And third, the site appears undisturbed, making it a kind of time capsule of its day. The reply to Stevens's report is both speedy and troubling.

Office of Information
Government House
Cherubia

December 12, 1984
Mr. J. Stevens, Director
Maritime Archaeological Research
c/o Overland University
Twine, Kansas
U.S.A.

Dear Mr. Stevens,

Many thanks for your most timely report. I regret to inform you that during the summer following your survey, treasure hunters were intercepted in the Brazos area. While I cannot say what, if any, damage may have been done, we in this office do not wish to lose a valuable source of historical information and a potential tourist attraction to the hands of such pirates. We are prepared, therefore, to engage your organization to excavate the site at your earliest convenience. In addition to paying your normal fees, we are also able to provide a ship that could serve as the base of operations on the site. Mr. Morp would once again serve as our representative. Please let me know whether or not you will be able to undertake this project.

Cordially,

Wendell Manatu
Deputy Director

A sense of urgency brought about by the specter of treasure hunters now reinforces the desire to excavate, already fueled by the handful of clues. Because of uncertainties about the size and difficulty of the project, planning is undertaken for an initial three-month investigation. Joining Stevens, Sousa, and Keiffer will be MAR members Jeff Armet, Rocky Waitz, and Diane Lacey along with five graduate students from the university. Everything from inflatable boats and diving tanks to milk crates and plastic sandwich bags is assembled and checked. Two months later, as the equipment is being loaded for the trip to Miami, a fax arrives from Lacey in Seville, Spain.

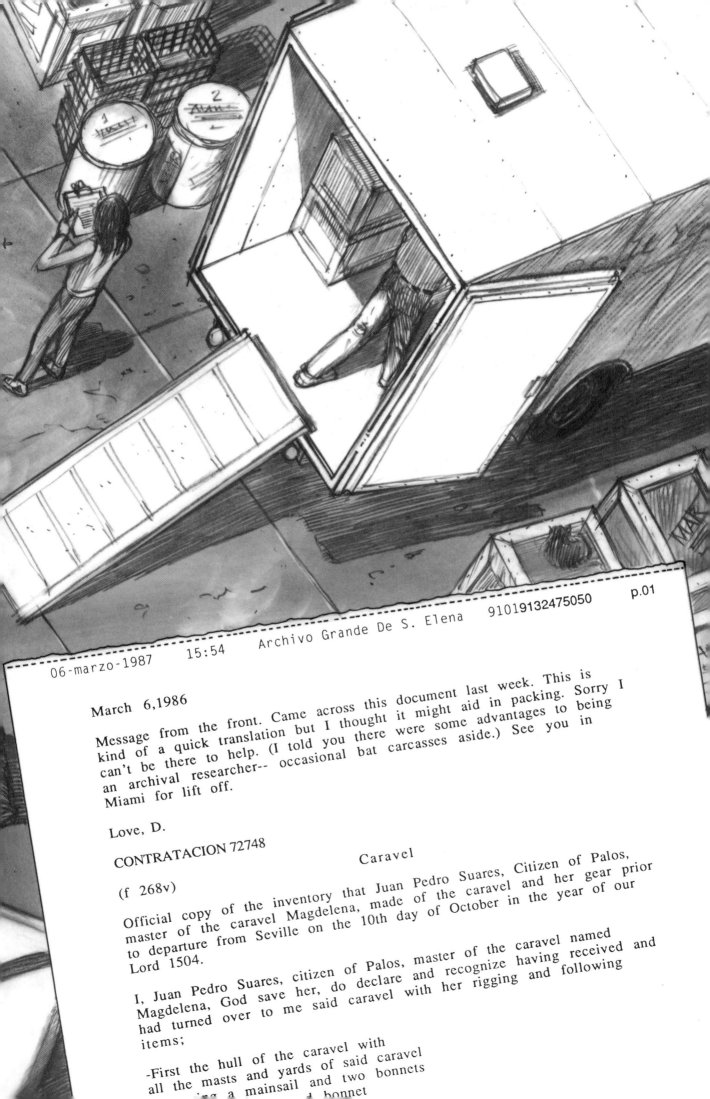

March 6,1986

Message from the front. Came across this document last week. This is kind of a quick translation but I thought it might aid in packing. Sorry I can't be there to help. (I told you there were some advantages to being an archival researcher-- occasional bat carcasses aside.) See you in Miami for lift off.

Love, D.

CONTRATACION 72748

Caravel

(f 268v)

Official copy of the inventory that Juan Pedro Suares, Citizen of Palos, master of the caravel Magdelena, made of the caravel and her gear prior to departure from Seville on the 10th day of October in the year of our Lord 1504.

I, Juan Pedro Suares, citizen of Palos, master of the caravel named Magdelena, God save her, do declare and recognize having received and had turned over to me said caravel with her rigging and following items;

-First the hull of the caravel with all the masts and yards of said caravel ~~~~~~~ a mainsail and two bonnets ~~~~~ bonnet

On the first and second of April, everything required for the trip is transferred to a well-worn Cherubian ship, *Pride of the Sea*. Early on the morning of the third, this floating "home away from home" weighs anchor.

Five days later, Stevens and Keiffer witness the carnage. The anchor that had first welcomed them to the site has been torn away, leaving only scars in the sea bed. A swivel gun lies in pieces, apparently not worth the effort of retrieval after being shattered. All along the path smaller artifacts are either missing or have been moved. Braced for the worst, the two men cross the reef and for a few moments just stare. Fragments of timber and broken gorgonia surround a gaping hole near one end of the ballast mound. Once again, in their frenzied search for anything shiny, treasure hunters have destroyed whatever got in their way. The accuracy with which the site had been recorded during the archaeologist's first visit is now more important than ever.

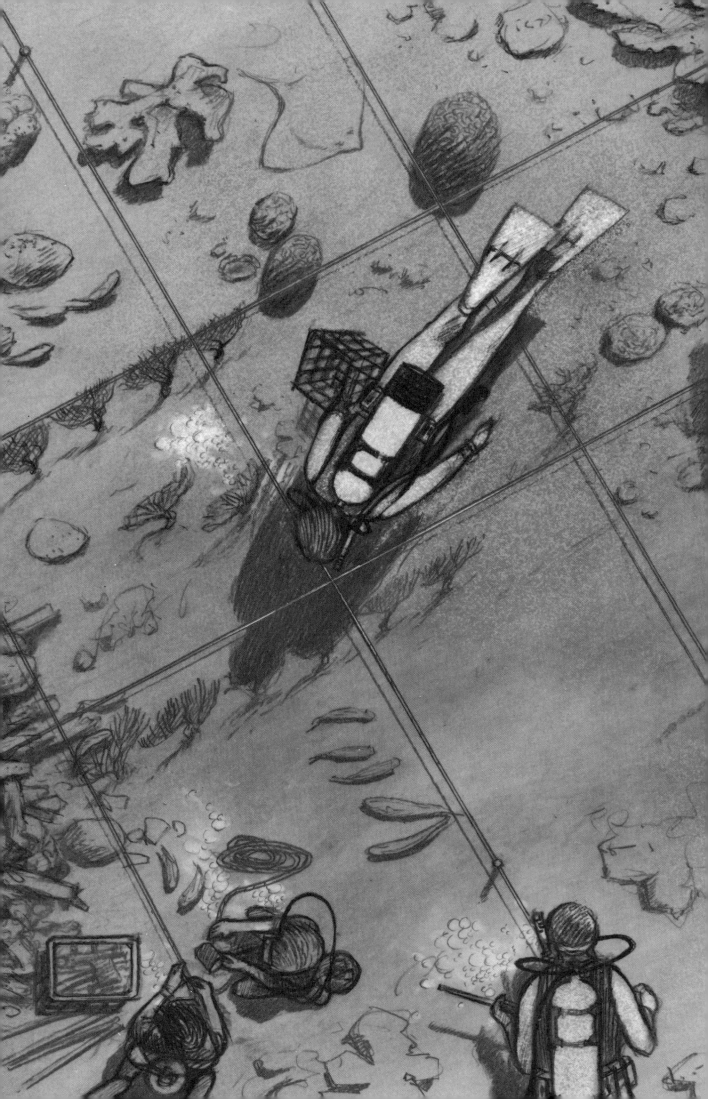

Stevens divides the groups into two teams. One will produce a more precise plan recording everything within a quarter mile of the wreck site. The other will secure a rope grid over the ballast area and scatter site to help in recording the exact locations of everything uncovered.

To determine the extent of the wooden remains without having to remove all the ballast, three trenches will be dug, one across the center of the mound and one each at the suspected bow and stern of the wreck. The area damaged by the treasure hunters will be avoided. Before any excavation begins, formations of coral and sponge are carefully removed. At the completion of the dig they will be returned to their original places to help minimize disruption of the reef environment.

Sand and fragments of dead coral that cover the area to be excavated are sucked up into a curved plastic pipe and carried away through a long flexible hose. Two divers sift through the sand before it disappears. Each fragment of pottery or glass is placed in its own plastic bag and numbered. Eventually, two large artifacts come into view at the center of the mound. One is an anchor and the other is a cannon called a bombardeta. Both are tagged, photographed, and drawn in place.

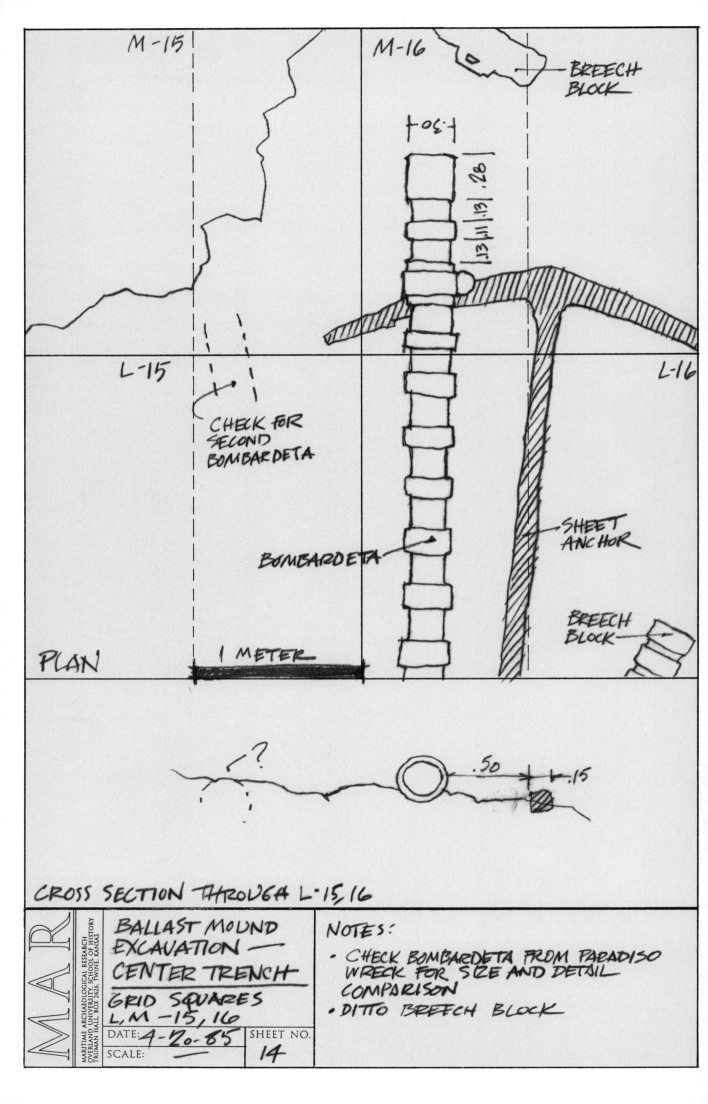

M-15

M-16

BREECH
BLOCK

L-15

CHECK FOR
SECOND
BOMBARDETA

L-16

BOMBARDETA

SHEET
ANCHOR

BREECH
BLOCK

PLAN

1 METER

?

.50

.15

CROSS SECTION THROUGH L-15,16

BALLAST MOUND
EXCAVATION —
CENTER TRENCH

GRID SQUARES
L, M -15, 16

DATE: 4-20-85

SCALE: ——

SHEET NO.
14

NOTES:

- CHECK BOMBARDETA FROM PARADISO
  WRECK FOR SIZE AND DETAIL
  COMPARISON
- DITTO BREECH BLOCK

All measurements must be accurately recorded on both plans and sections every step of the way, because as the site is being systematically excavated, it is also being changed forever.

Once the artifacts are chiseled free, they are lifted off their stony beds and transferred to a holding area beyond the grid. They will remain there until the end of the dig. Smaller artifacts are taken to the mother ship in milk crates at the end of each day.

During the following three weeks of ten-hour days, ballast stones and artifacts, including a second bombardeta, are removed from the three trenches. As the ship's fragile wooden remains are gradually exposed, they are immediately covered by sandbags and sand to protect them from the current and accidental damage until they can be precisely recorded.

Every evening after dinner, Maria Sousa painstakingly traces the small plans made under water onto a single large sheet. This master plan will be updated throughout the life of the excavation — both at sea and back in the lab.

Toward the end of May, Stevens moves most of the crew to the scatter site to recover objects detected during the survey. The majority are guns, breech chambers, and shot. Closer to the timbers, and in many cases still holding them together, a variety of metal fasteners are recovered. From among the ballast stones, more pieces of glass, pottery fragments, and the encrusted head of a carpenter's adze emerge. While the search for new artifacts continues, one archaeologist is assigned to each of the three trenches to make detailed drawings.

For Diane Lacey, June 17 begins like every other day. Out of her slightly damp bunk into a slightly damp bathing suit for a slightly soggy breakfast. Then into a slightly damp wet suit before loading equipment into the small boats and setting off for the untold pleasures of the scatter site. But it doesn't end like every other day. Late that afternoon, while diving for lobsters about a mile southwest of the wreck site, Lacey comes across the concreted hilt of a dagger, and peeking out from just beneath it, a small gold cross. While there is no reason to believe these artifacts are connected in any way to the Brazos wreck, it is definitely everyone's first choice. Having undergone two and a half months of uninterrupted excavation, the wreck still has not given up even a single possession belonging to one of its ill-fated crew.

Around the dinner table that evening, two questions keep coming up. Could these objects be linked to the wreck? And if so, since neither of them floats, how did they get so far away? Following much spirited discussion, Armet suggests that some or all of the crew might have tried to escape their doomed ship in the ship's boat. Most likely overloaded, the boat could easily have capsized, especially in conditions violent enough to force a large ship onto the reef. A third question emerges. If Armet's scenario is correct, might there not be other artifacts in the area?

With only eleven days left, pressure is building to complete the work already started. Can the team afford the time to investigate a second site, which, in spite of its appeal, might ultimately have nothing to do with the first? On the other hand, what if those artifacts can be tied to the crew of their wreck? And supposing just one of them had a date on it?

By seven o'clock the following morning, Lacey and Waitz are back on what is optimistically referred to as the "capsize site" armed with metal detectors. In less than two hours they locate a wrought-iron swivel gun called a haquebut, part of a crossbow, a navigational instrument called an astrolabe, and a small anchor. Enough of the right kinds of things are turning up to strengthen the capsize theory, so the next four days are spent recording the area in detail.

Meanwhile, back at the main site, large artifacts that have been kept on the sea bed to protect them from the air are now hoisted onto the deck of the mother ship. Every effort is made during the final week to recover all metal artifacts, since they are the things most likely to attract more treasure hunters. Although a few fragments are taken for analysis, most of the wooden remains are reburied. Their recovery will be a long and even more painstaking process and will have to wait for another visit.

On July 5, *Pride of the Sea* sails toward Miami with its precious cargo and weary passengers.

By the end of the month, everyone has readjusted to a floor that doesn't move, dry clothes, and friendly food. The artifacts are soaking in tanks of solution to reduce deterioration caused by salt water. Like anything removed from one environment and thrust into another, each object recovered from the Brazos reef, whether wood, metal, ceramic, glass, or

SOAKING   CLEANING   ELECTROLYSIS

stone, requires great care and plenty of time if it is going to adapt and survive. Since iron artifacts such as guns and anchors deteriorate quickly if not properly preserved, and because they are among the most likely items to be identified with a mark or date, they are the first to undergo treatment.

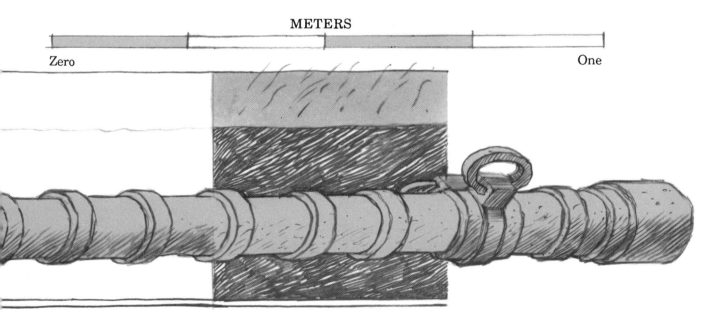

METERS

Zero   One

BATH   WAX EMERSION   FINISHED ARTIFACT

For most of the artifacts, cleaning and preserving takes months and sometimes years. Occasionally, however, the deterioration either cannot be stopped or has already gone too far when the item is discovered. In this case the encrustation often serves as a mold from which a replica of the original can be cast.

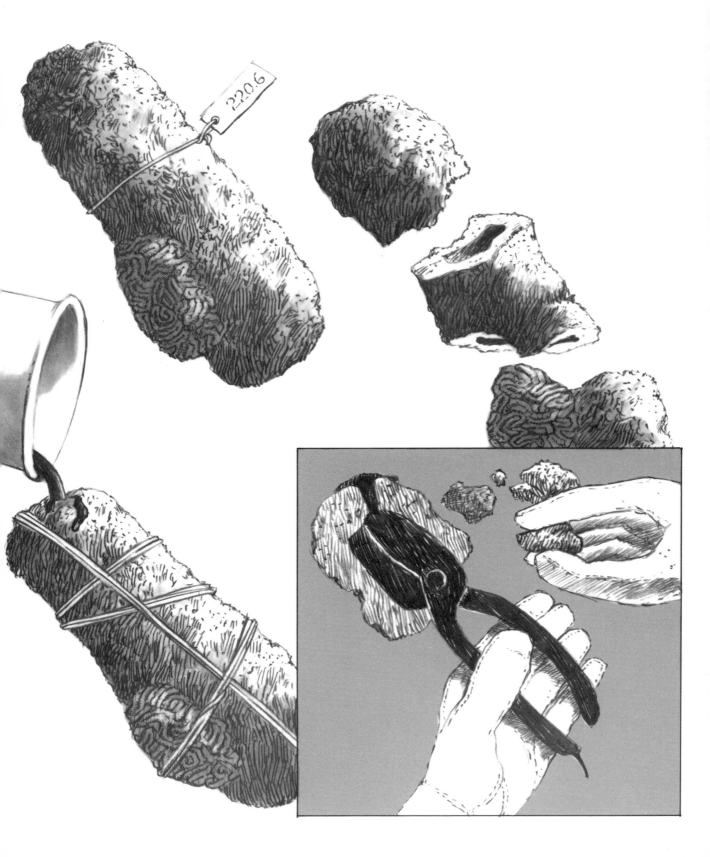

Over the centuries, many of the thousands of artifacts, including the nails, bolts, and tacks that once held the ship together, have become cemented into large clusters called conglomerates. Just as the location of each conglomerate is recorded on the site plan, so the location of each artifact within a conglomerate must also be carefully recorded.

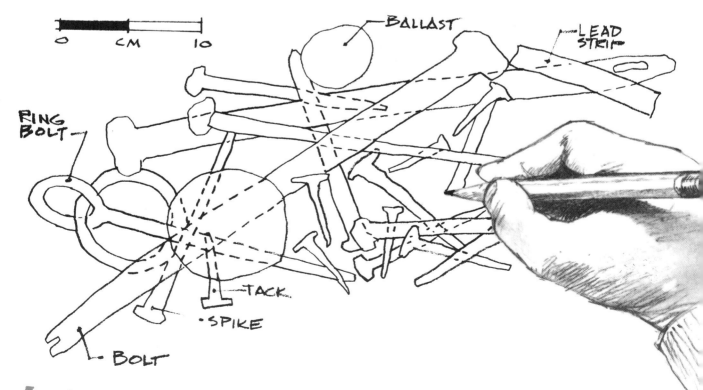

BALLAST

LEAD STRIP

RING BOLT

TACK

SPIKE

BOLT

0   CM   10

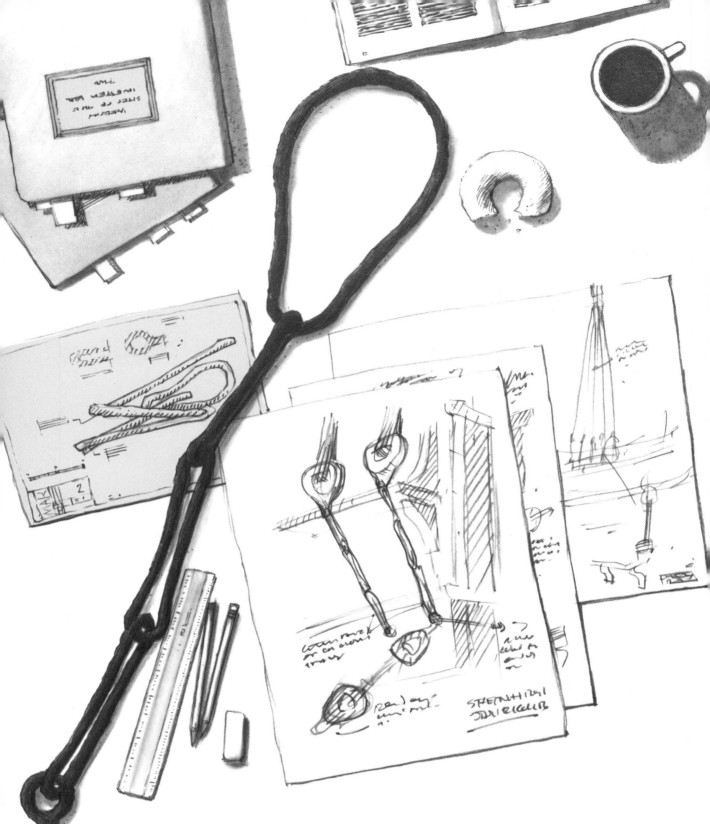

Occasionally stopping to dip his doughnut into a cup of hot black coffee as if it were an artifact getting its wax coating, Jack Stevens contemplates a wrought-iron chain found at the bow of the ship. Similar artifacts have been uncovered at other sixteenth-century sites and even appear in a few pictures from that time. They are that part of the ship's standing rigging which connects the ropes from the top of a mast to the sides of the hull below. The presence of this hardware indicates that the ship was fitted with at least one square sail, an increasingly popular addition to transatlantic vessels by the end of the fifteenth century.

Because no coins or documentary evidence has yet turned up to identify the ship's port of origin, Rocky Waitz studies samples of the perma-
nent ballast. These large stones, found at the bottom of the pile, would
have been placed on board around the time of the launch. They turn out
to be identical to types of stone still found on the Iberian Peninsula in
both Spain and Portugal. The uppermost layer of stones, and therefore
the most recent additions to the pile, includes pieces of coral that must
have been picked up somewhere in the Caribbean. This suggests that
cargo had recently been unloaded, leaving the ship in need of extra
weight to maintain stability. There is no indication of what that cargo
may have been, although known possibilities include dyewood, cacao,
pearls, and slaves. Perhaps one clue lies in the fact that the ship sank
with many of its swivel guns loaded. Was this a precaution taken to
protect a valuable cargo or a decision made to help in acquiring a reluc-
tant one?

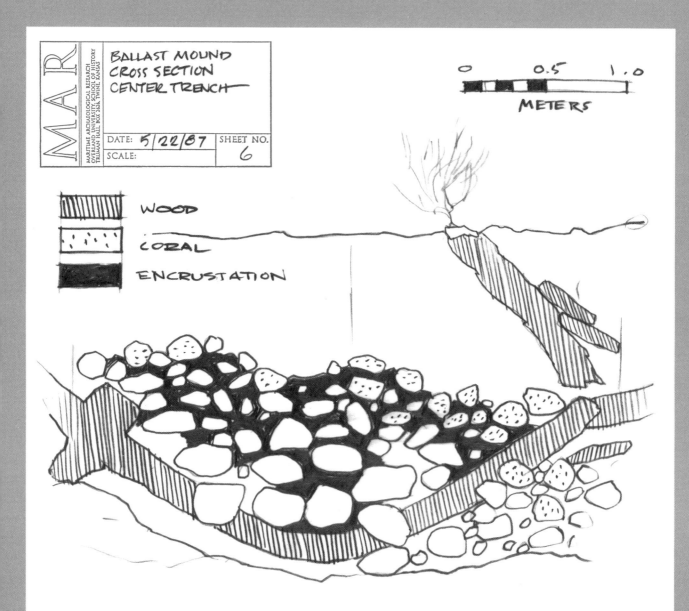

BALLAST MOUND
CROSS SECTION
CENTER TRENCH

MAR
MARITIME ARCHAEOLOGICAL RESEARCH
OVERLAND UNIVERSITY, SCHOOL OF HISTORY
TRUMAN HALL, BOX 2424, TWINE, KANSAS

DATE: 5/22/87   SHEET NO. 6
SCALE:

0   0.5   1.0
METERS

WOOD
CORAL
ENCRUSTATION

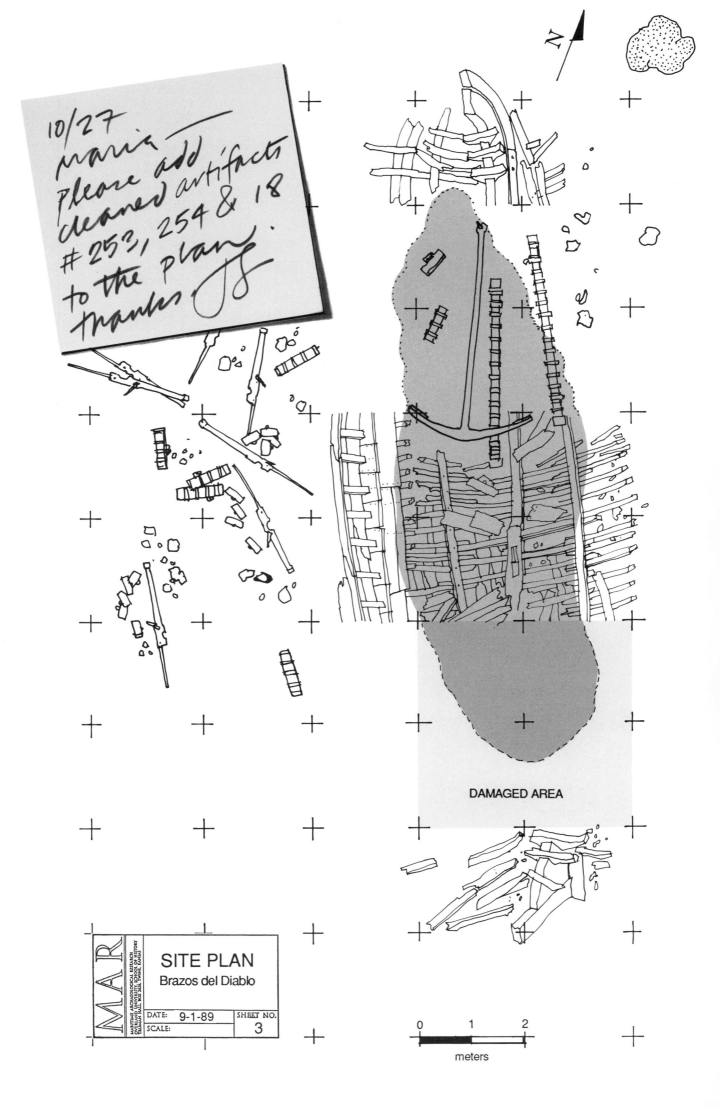

10/27
maria —
please add
cleaned artifacts
#253, 254 & 18
to the plan.
thanks. JG

N

DAMAGED AREA

SITE PLAN
Brazos del Diablo

MAR
MARITIME ARCHAEOLOGICAL RESEARCH
OVERLAND UNIVERSITY, SCHOOL OF HISTORY
TRUMAN HALL, BOX 5454, TOWNE, KANSAS

DATE: 9-1-89   SHEET NO.
SCALE: 3

0   1   2

meters

Over the next five years, two more trips are made to the site during which more artifacts, including all the wooden remains, are recovered. Before long, however, information that will help interpret them is coming from well beyond the Brazos del Diablo reef and the archives of Seville. Hundreds of additional details about construction and rigging continue to emerge from wrecks being excavated by other archaeologists, not only in the Caribbean and the Gulf of Mexico but as far away as Canada and England.

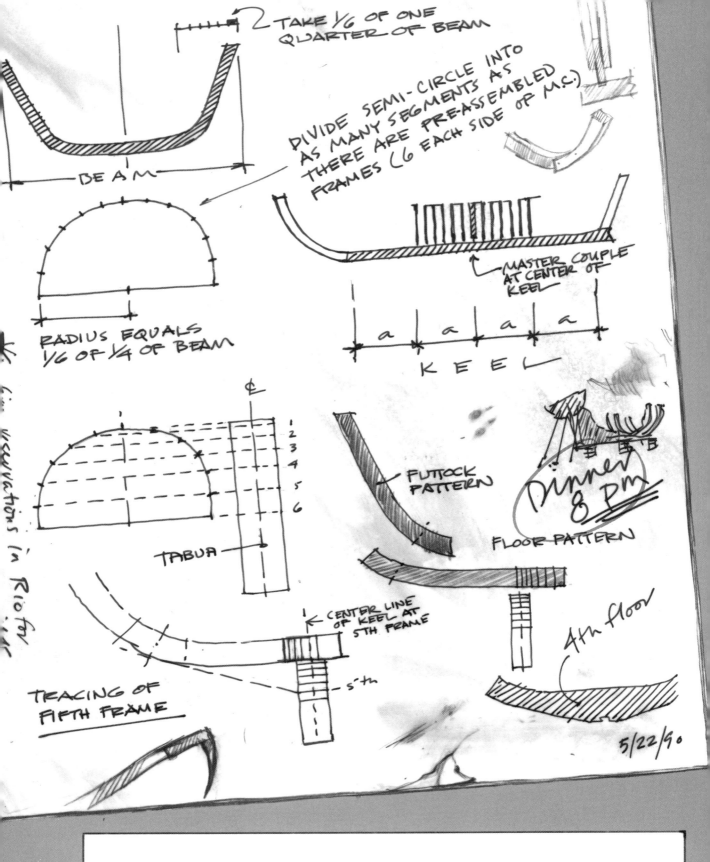

TAKE 1/6 OF ONE QUARTER OF BEAM

BEAM

DIVIDE SEMI-CIRCLE INTO AS MANY SEGMENTS AS THERE ARE PRE-ASSEMBLED FRAMES (6 EACH SIDE OF M.C.)

RADIUS EQUALS 1/6 OF 1/4 OF BEAM

MASTER COUPLE AT CENTER OF KEEL

a   a   a   a

KEEL

₵

1
2
3
4
5
6

TABUA

FUTTOCK PATTERN

Dinner 8 PM

FLOOR PATTERN

CENTER LINE OF KEEL AT 5TH FRAME

5th

4th floor

TRACING OF FIFTH FRAME

5/22/90

observations in Rio for

For a firsthand look at five-hundred-year-old shipbuilding techniques, several members of the team visit boatyards in the Brazilian state of Bahia where they are still being practiced. The archaeologists are particularly interested in the creation and use of wooden patterns to establish the shape of a ship's hull, as well as types of tools, all of which survive from the earliest days of sixteenth-century Portuguese exploration.

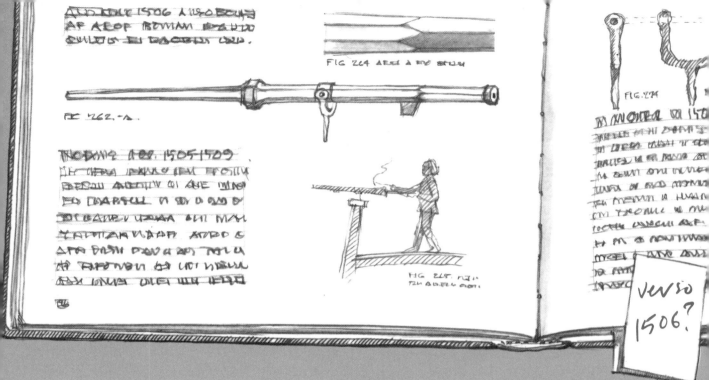

As the number of identified artifacts grows, so does the likelihood of accurately dating the ship that carried them. Guns from the wreck, most likely made in the Low Countries, are compared with examples in various Dutch and Belgian museums. The haquebut found at the capsize site is identical to those in use between 1415 and 1515.

Several small Spanish bowls are reconstructed from fragments found in the ballast mound. Their shape, clay color, and kind of glaze identify them as a style of bowl that is known to have been out of use by around 1520. Other fragments come from pottery made by the native population of Lucayos, a group of Caribbean islands. Historians have determined that shortly after the arrival of Europeans in the New World, the Lucayan Arawak population was decimated. It is unlikely that they made anything, including pottery, after about 1513.

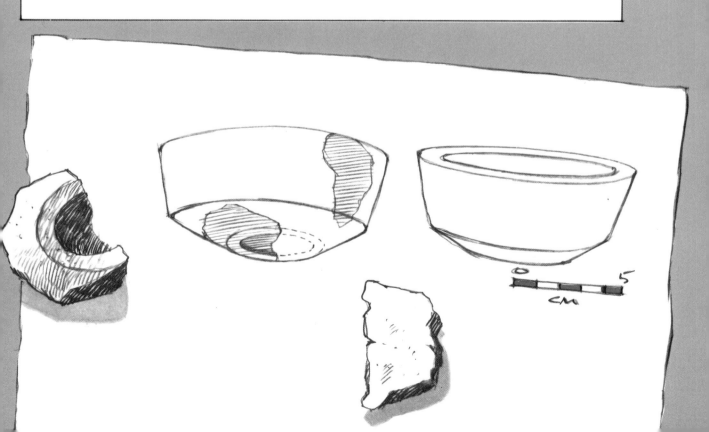

The patient on the worktable this afternoon is artifact S53, the bronze astrolabe from the capsize site. As chips of encrustation fall away, the numbers *1* and *5* come into view. Armet lets out an uncharacteristic "Yeehaw!" and attracts the attention of everyone in the lab. Only the cat seems uninterested. Sousa, Stevens, Waitz, and Keiffer soon hover over the worktable like medical students observing their first triple-bypass operation. Another centimeter of stony skin is removed, but the surface below is seriously scarred. A second centimeter of encrustation crumbles below the chisel to reveal the faint but unmistakable lines of a *4*. Ten eyes focus on the pitted area between the *5* and the *4*, hunting for traces of the missing digit or perhaps trying to will it back into existence. But *15 4* is as much information as the astrolabe willingly surrenders.

That evening, as thunderstorms roll over Twine, Kansas, Jack Stevens puts the finishing touches on an article for the popular magazine *Wet History*.

IN THE ARMS OF THE DEVIL
or, The Last Moments of a Sixteenth Century Caravel
by
J. R. Stevens

One day between 1504 and 1514 a heavily armed caravel was sailing in the Caribbean one hundred fifty miles due west of the Cherubian Islands. To the east, a string of dark clouds that had clung to the horizon for much of the afternoon was beginning to grow. Gradually, the air around the small ship thickened, becoming almost too heavy and hot to breathe. By the time the first gusts tore at the sails, the hatches, ship's boat, extra yards and swivel guns had been secured. Everything else was stowed below. Almost instantly, a few drops of rain turned into sheets of water pounding the deck and everyone on it. Bursts of lightning directly overhead transformed the frantic scene into a series of eerie stills. Tossing helplessly between the glistening mountains of a raging landscape, the ship seemed to grow smaller and smaller.

A shout from the top of the mainmast warned of the nearby reef. Immediately, the captain ordered one of the bower anchors dropped. When it failed to hold, a second followed, only to be dragged along the bottom. Crewmen struggled in the dark and against the crashing waves to lash together four swivel guns that were then thrown overboard to serve as a makeshift anchor. But nothing could prevent the ship from careening toward the black foaming waters. A sudden thud from deep below threw everyone to the watery deck. Spitting out sea water and blood, their eyes stung by the force of the salty spray, the crew crawled across the slippery planks, clearing the deck of guns and shot in an attempt to float the ship over its hidden enemy. But the waves continued to drag the helpless vessel back and forth over the reef's razor-sharp teeth, grinding away more timber with each pass.

In one last effort to further lighten the ship and to prevent the keel from snapping, the main yard was lowered and tossed overboard, sail and all. The mate and one of the ship's carpenters chopped down the mainmast. It, too, disappeared into the deep. But the voracious appetite of the murderous reef would not be satisfied. Pieces of planking were now being torn from their ribs. As ballast spilled out, water poured in. The pump men could no longer keep up. Mortally wounded, the ship began to list.

Clutching a few personal possessions and whatever food and supplies they could manage, those who could abandoned ship, the luckiest ones clambering aboard the ship's boat. Into the unknown they rowed with all their might, away from the reef that had terrorized them, away from the tangled remains of their only link with home, away from the anguished cries of those still lost in the darkness. After traveling less than a mile, the boat was hit broadside by a sudden wave and capsized, tossing its passengers and all their possessions into the sea.

The following morning, a few exhausted men desperately clung to anything that floated—an oar, the boat's mast, even the boat itself. But there was neither drinking water nor food, and even the astrolabe by which they might have charted a course had been claimed by the sea. Soon the sun would sit high above them, draining their last ounces of bodily fluid, while enemies of a different sort waited patiently below. There was nothing left but prayer and the remote possibility of a passing ship. At this moment, they were at the mercy of Nature and a current that might eventually deliver them to the northern shore of Cuba. There, a tribe of natives, whose dietary customs were the subject of terrifying tales, were waiting.

November 7, 1993

Fellow Diggers,

Greetings and bingo from fair Seville. I have found what looks like a journal or diary inside a bundle of early-sixteenth-century legal papers. At first I thought it was just another case of creative filing, but it seems, after a quick read, that both are somehow connected to a shipyard owned by a family named Guerra. I translated a document three years ago giving a Señora Guerra, the widow of a deceased shipyard owner, official custody of her own children. Maybe they're related. Don't know yet. But here's the great news. The first couple of entries seem to be specifically about the building of a caravel. I'll read them as quickly as I can but the handwriting is worse than Rocky's. Just kidding, Rock.

See you soon. Love,

Diane

Nobel Prize Committee
Stockholm, Sweden

TWINE ELECTRIC COMPANY
645 PRAIRIE LANE
TWINE, KANSAS

Maritime Arch
Box 4008, Shaw
Twine, Kansas

The Seventh day of January in the year of Our Lord – 1504 –

Although my brother Garcia and I are presently enjoying great success importing dyewood and pearls from the Indies, it seems only prudent to be searching for new sources of these precious commodities before we run out (or someone else finds them). We have therefore commissioned the building of a caravel. Such a ship, although quite small, is surprisingly capacious. It is also of modest draft and can be heavily armed, making it ideal for the uncertainties of exploration.

This latest addition to the Vergara fleet is to be built by the Guerra shipyard, which continues to flourish under the watchful eye of the widow Guerra. Prices remain high, but so too does the quality of the work, all of which is overseen by master shipwright Alonso de Fonseca. Because my personal life in Seville has grown somewhat complicated, Garcia has agreed that I should sail with the ship on its maiden voyage. For my own piece of mind, therefore, I have taken it upon myself to observe and record all aspects of the vessel's construction.

The Ninth day of January

Master Alonso looks favorably upon my quest and promises
that no detail shall be overlooked. We passed this rainy afternoon
reviewing the list of timbers required for the hull, all of which, I am
pleased to report, will be the finest white oak. Once a year, Alonso
and his master carpenter, José de Arbora, visit the forests to select
lumber for their ships. In the winter, the trees they have marked are
felled and sent on their way.

The Eleventh day of January

Alonso, José, and I passed much of this morning with two lumber merchants who were attempting to justify their high prices. They complained incessantly about the difficulty of transporting wood to the city. Alonso countered their claims by suggesting that the Guadalquivir River does all the work. "It flows directly from the mountains to the sea and passes right by our shipyard on its way. All you have to do is throw the logs in and, two hundred miles later, pull them out!"

The Eighteenth day of January

By the time I reached the yard, José and his able apprentices were already shaping the keel—the very backbone of our ship, which, incidentally, we have named *Magdalena*. "Once the rough shape has been established with the ax," he informed me, "each face of the timber will be smoothed with the short strokes of the adze." José is reputed to be one of the finest adze men in the city, although his apprenticeship was not without personal cost. His right foot carries only four toes.

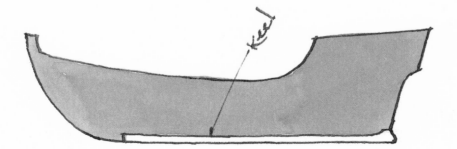

the thirtieth day of January

Not surprisingly, my arrival this morning was greeted with greater than usual enthusiasm. As the sun, which has been rare of late, added its blessing to that of the good friar, *Magdalena*'s finished keel was levered up and onto its supports. This event, according to our contract, marks the day upon which my brother and I are bound to pay the first of three sums of money to the shipyard. This we did at the inn, in the presence of Alonso and the Señora's eldest son, Diego. After toasting the continued success of our venture, Master Alonso bade me accompany him to the blacksmith's. There he ordered large quantities of iron nails and bolts as well as two dozen spikes almost the length of my arm.

The Fifteenth day of February

The curved stempost that will lead *Magdalena* through the waves is now secured to the keel. A generous coating of pitch was applied to the adjoining surfaces before they were permanently fastened—a procedure that, Alonso assures me, will be repeated throughout construction to prevent rot. This afternoon a large curved brace called a deadwood was hoisted onto the keel where it fit with perfection into the curve of the stempost.

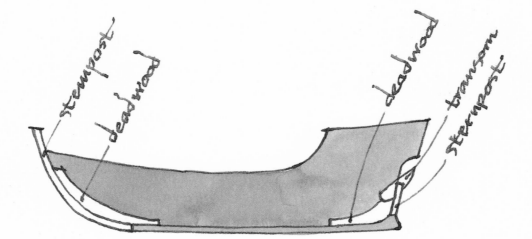

The Twenty-ninth day of February

The yard is very busy these days, and Alonso has been much distracted. One of Their Royal Highnesses' ships has been hauled over onto its side for repairs to the hull, and the cargo vessel that sits next to *Magdalena* is already being caulked in preparation for its launch. At the opposite end of *Magdalena*'s keel from the stempost, the sternpost and its deadwood are now in place. Together they support a fine broad transom. As I was leaving the yard, I found Alonso threatening one of the lumber merchants with all manner of legal retribution if the merchant did not immediately provide the promised timbers. "Did the Lord create lumber merchants simply to impede the shipwright's progress?" he shouted. "It is truly a miracle that Noah finished his work in time and that we were not all lost to the Great Flood."

From *Magdalena*'s sturdy spine, her ribs must now be built. After making a series of complicated calculations, which, he tells me, all begin with the length of the keel, Alonso creates two patterns from which all the largest ribs will be traced. Every rib is to be built in three pieces. The bottommost section, called the floor, will sit directly on the keel or deadwoods. Secured to the ends of each floor are the futtocks, which will support the sides of the ship. By slightly adjusting the pieces of the pattern for each one, Alonso and his apprentices trace the shapes of the first thirteen ribs.

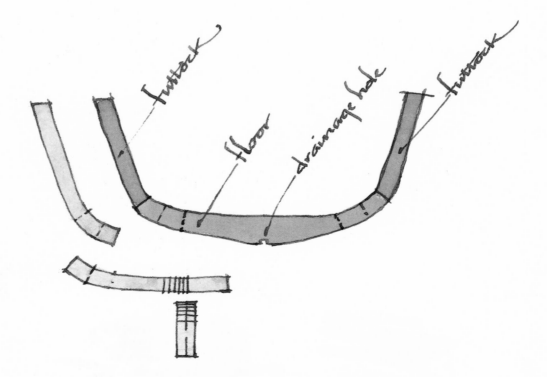

The Twentieth day of March

It has been some time since I put pen to paper. I was confined to my bed for two weeks with a terrible fever, although now, thanks be to God, I have regained my strength. Much has happened in my absence. The cargo ship that once stood next to *Magdalena* has been launched and now awaits its masts. Not only is our vessel free from its shadow, but the first of *Magdalena*'s ribs have been assembled and hoisted into place on the keel.

Because all ships, even those built by Alonso de Fonseca, are bound to leak, he has instructed that a small notch be cut at the base of each floor to direct water to the pump. I can tell you, having personally ventured into the holds of ships where this refinement was overlooked, the result is a most foul-smelling stew.

The Twenty-second day of March

This morning Alonso, José, and two apprentices began tacking thin strips of wood called ribbands between the posts and ribs on one side of the ship. Only after several hours of adjusting and readjusting did the two master craftsmen seem satisfied with the resulting shape. The curvature of each ribband was then carefully measured so that it could be replicated exactly on the opposite side of the ship. When all the ribbands are in place, a pattern will be made for each remaining rib.

The Twenty-fourth day of March

The keelson, an impressive piece of timber, is now installed. It rests upon the ribs directly above the keel. Because of its size and great weight, it was slipped into the hull before all the futtocks were attached.

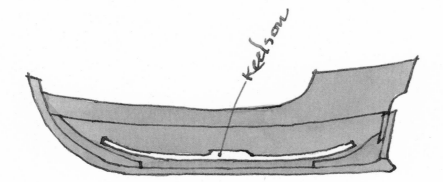

Easter Week

When the last of the ribs are in place, the tops of each futtock are then tied together by two heavy planks called wales. Each wale has been slowly bent over a hot fire so that it follows the curvature of the hull. Starting at the stempost on one side of the ship, carpenters move along the scaffolding, first drilling holes and then securing each connection with both iron nails and wooden pegs called treenails. It is José's desire to install both wales before the Easter fair, since leaving only one in place, even for a week, could cause the entire frame to become twisted.

The Twenty-fourth day of April

The keelson is notched to fit snugly over every floor and is held in place with long iron spikes. The wooden skeleton is further secured by two additional pieces of timber called stringers. These, too, are notched and extend from bow to stern along both sides of the keelson.

The Twenty-seventh day of April

Garcia chided me today for spending too much time at the shipyard. We have three ships leaving within the month, and there are still contracts to be drawn up and supplies to be gathered. I can barely force myself to confront the endless columns of figures that cover the pages of our ledgers, but as my elder brother points out, it is those endless columns which are paying for my current pleasure.

It appears that Alonso has finally conquered the lumber men. Wood arrives every day, and much of it is immediately dragged to the saw pits for cutting. Piles of planks now lay waiting along both sides of the ship. José's carpenters have been sheathing the hull below the wales. They painstakingly measure and trim each plank to create the tightest possible seam before drilling and securing it to the ribs.

The Twenty-eighth day of May

Curved beams required to support the deck and ensure its drainage are now in place. José has begun framing a large hatch in the center of the deck so that cargo can be easily stored below. To increase the amount of deck space and provide some protection from the elements, a second, smaller deck is under construction at the stern.

the thirty-first day of May

I was introduced today to Vincente Albene, a master caulker. He and his crew will seal the hull and later the deck by pounding strands of tar-soaked hemp called oakum into every seam. As a further precaution against leakage, Master Alonso has asked that a thin strip of lead be tacked over the oakum in those seams which will lie below the water line. No matter how well Albene does his work, however, some water will most certainly find its way into the hold. To return it to the sea as quickly as possible, Alonso has installed a pump that rises from the depths of the hold up through the main deck.

the twenty-third day of June

The past two days have been spent getting ready for the launch. Once Albene and Alonso were satisfied with the caulking, the hull was coated with pitch. *Magdalena* was then carefully lowered onto two parallel wooden tracks that extend to the river. Tomorrow they will be covered with a thick coating of animal fat to help the ship slide more easily. The keel will travel freely in a trench dug between the tracks. This afternoon Alonso supervised the placement of many stones on the floor of the hold to help steady the ship as it enters the water.

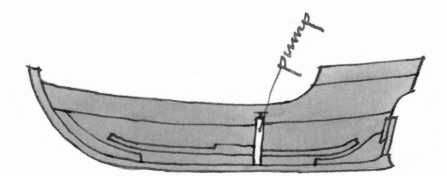

The Twenty-fourth day of June

At about two o'clock Alonso gave the order from the bow to remove the remaining supports. At first there was no movement. Then, as people along both sides gently rocked the hull, it gradually slid onto the greased portion of the tracks. Cheers filled the air as the ship glided whole into the same river that only a few months earlier had delivered her in pieces.

the Twenty-sixth day of June

My head has only just cleared enough so that I may continue
my account of *Magdalena*'s glorious birth. Even before the vessel was
docked, Alonso was at work in the hold, making minor adjustments to
the ballast. By the time we returned to the yard some two hours later,
it was evident from the exuberance of the celebration that my brother
had already complied with our contractual obligations and made the
second payment to the Guerra shipyard.

The Fourth day of July

The carpenters have attached the rudder and the tiller by which it is turned. While the four mast timbers are undergoing final preparations, José is building an officers' privy beneath the rear deck. "Why they cannot simply hang off the rails like the rest of the crew," he said to one of his apprentices, "I swear I do not know." Under the same rear deck, to either side of the tiller, he is also building two tiny cabins.

The Eighth day of July

Knowing that work would start while the air was still cool, I arrived shortly after sunrise to see the mainmast being raised above its hole in the center of the deck. This great pine trunk, straight and free of cracks, is as long as the keel. I quickly ran below deck and, just before the mast was lowered into its slot in the mast step, inserted a coin to bring us luck. Since I am to sail aboard *Magdalena,* it was of course a gold coin.

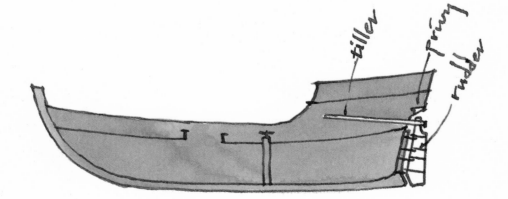

The twelfth day of July

All four masts are now in place. This morning Alonso turned *Magdalena* over to the master rigger, Alphon Sanchez. "Though he is older than me," Alonso said as he introduced us, "he can still out-climb and out-splice even his youngest apprentices."

The seventeenth day of July

Upon my arrival at the ship, coils of rope covered the deck and Alphon was high atop the mainmast attaching those pieces of the standing rigging, called shrouds, by which the masts are secured to the hull. (Incidentally, the rope we are using is made here in Seville, from only the finest hemp. I am certain of this because it is our cousins who import this material and the Señora's brother who twists it into its final form.)

Because of their tendency to stretch, the fixed lines of the rigging, particularly the shrouds, must frequently be tightened. To simplify this process, Alphon loops the bottom end of each shroud around a wooden block called a deadeye. A second deadeye is fastened by an iron chain to the side of the hull. By threading a thinner piece of rope between the deadeyes and drawing them together, tension can easily be maintained.

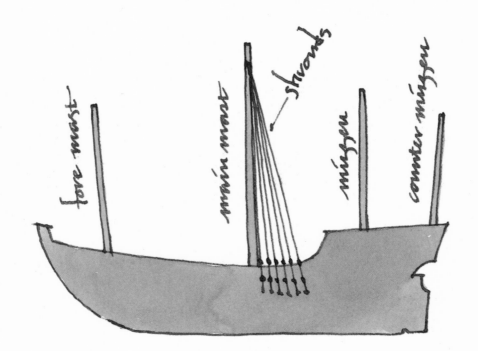

the seventh day of August

I visited the shipyard this morning hoping to see Alonso, but found instead a new keel on the very spot where *Magdalena* had stood less than a month ago. At midday, on my way to the warehouse, I came upon Alonso and José on the bridge, where we braved the traffic to discuss the speed with which *Magdalena's* standing rigging has come along. Not only are the shrouds of all four masts in place, but so are the much heavier stays of the mainmast and foremast.

the thirteenth day of August

The long horizontal yards, to which the sails will be attached, are made up of two pieces of timber bound together. Just this morning, Juan Gallanta, the sailmaker, stopped by to measure those already finished. At Alonso's suggestion, we have ordered two identical sets of sails for the ship, just in case, God forbid, there is an accident at sea.

Like his friend Alonso, Alphon wishes me to understand all that he is doing in order that I might fully appreciate the complexity of outfitting even a small ship like *Magdalena*. Whereas the standing rigging simply holds things in place, the running rigging serves to raise, lower, and adjust each of the sails so they make efficient use of the wind. To reduce wear, the lines of the running rigging travel over one or more wheels called sheaves, which are contained within wooden blocks called shells. The yards themselves are fastened to the masts with parrels—rings of wooden balls and slats designed to slide up and down with relative ease.

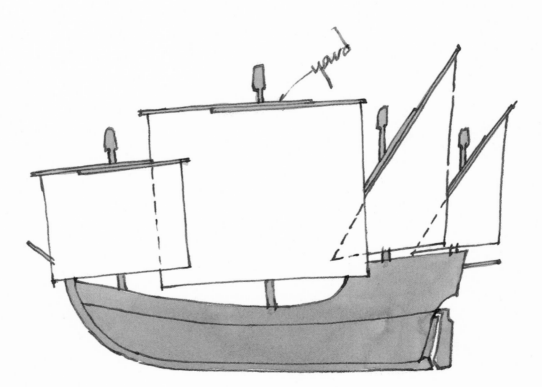

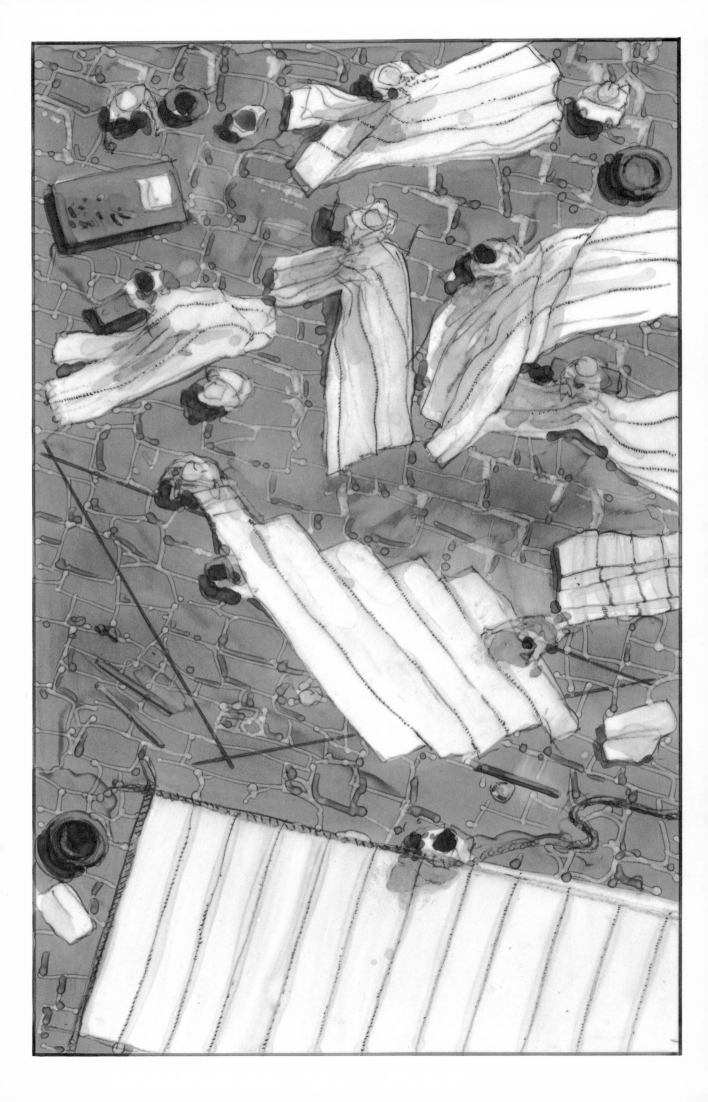

the Ninth day of september

Today, at Señor Gallanta's invitation, Garcia and I went to observe work on the sails and were much impressed. We first entered a storeroom in which bolts of strong French canvas line the shelves. A second door led into a large space where the strips of canvas are cut and stitched together to create the required shapes. Gallanta seems confident that his sails will tame even the strongest winds and carry our ship safely on its many journeys. I only hope he is right.

the seventeenth day of september

The shaft of the sheet anchor is more than twice my height. I marveled as the various pieces of iron of which it is made were heated in the red-hot coals of the forge and then pounded together on the anvil.

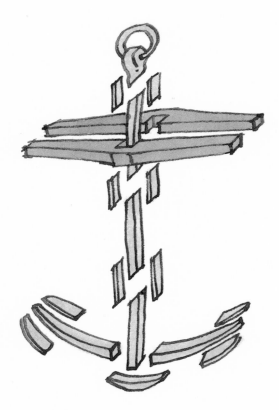

Twenty-third of September

I was on the dock inspecting a new shipment of dyewood when two wagons arrived bearing *Magdalena's* sails. One set was lashed to the yards, the other stowed below. The quartermaster, meanwhile, supervised the placement of supplies in the hold for the short journey down the Guadalquivir River to Sanlúcar de Barrameda, the port from which we will eventually set sail for the Indies. Pedro de Eguia, who will pilot *Magdalena*, was busy below the rear deck, checking each of the navigational tools and instruments of measurement with which, God willing, we will always know our place on His great sea.

Eighth day of October

This afternoon, shortly after the third and final payment was made to the Guerra shipyard, a complete inventory of the ship and all its contents was begun. Before we depart, it will be signed by our captain, Juan Pedro Suares, whose responsibility *Magdalena* now becomes.

Sixteenth day of October

We are ready to leave Seville at last. Both the Señora and Master Alonso were on hand to see us off. My brother Garcia and young Diego Guerra, having some business to attend to in Sanlúcar, will sail with us as far as the coast. I will entrust these notes to them prior to my departure from Spain.

Nineteenth day of October

We have arrived in Sanlúcar, a modest but pleasant town with a busy harbor, where Captain Suares has hired additional crewmen, bringing our number up to thirty. Although they seem a rough lot, he assures me they are reliable and experienced. A great many guns were brought aboard today. Most are swivel guns, which are to be mounted on the ship's rail. Two, however, are great long cannons called bombardetas. To keep the deck clear, they were immediately stored in the hold along with their wooden carriages and the great sheet anchor.

Thirtieth day of October

Once again, the quartermaster has been checking and rechecking his list of provisions as a steady procession of crates, sacks, and barrels passes down the gangway. Throughout the harbor, similar preparations are being made aboard the other four ships that will join *Magdalena* on its maiden voyage. Before leaving this afternoon, and in an uncharacteristic gesture of sentiment, Garcia presented me with a gold cross to ensure my safe return. (Or perhaps to guarantee my speedy departure?)

The Ninth day of November

Last-minute details and a lack of wind have kept us in port these past few days. But we are now ready to sail and our prayers for a fair wind have been answered. While I am eager to be on my way and have much confidence in Master Alonso's vessel, I would be speaking an untruth if I claimed I was not without some apprehension.

Two days ago I watched an old caravel as it rounded Punta de Motijo and drifted slowly into the mouth of the Guadalquivir. It was listing badly. The mainmast seemed to have been repaired at least once and the sails, although secure, had obviously been patched a number of times. I thought how strong and seaworthy *Magdalena* looked by comparison. That evening Captain Suares informed me that none other than Admiral Columbus himself was aboard that weary vessel, having just returned from the New World.

It was a humbling reminder, I can tell you, and brought about at least one extra visit to the church for prayers. Even in the hands of the most courageous and skillful sailors, all our ships, including *Magdalena*, are at the mercy of the Creator who has made the great ocean. I hope and pray He looks favorably upon our ship and its crew and that He will guide us safely back to this fair land.

Although a work of fiction, *Ship* is based almost entirely on recent and continuing
efforts of archaeologists and historians around the world. While it would be
impossible to thank them all, I wish to acknowledge a very special debt to five of
their colleagues at Ships of Exploration and Discovery Research
in Corpus Christi, Texas:
Donald Keith, Joe Simmons, Denise Lakey, Toni Carrell, and
Jerry Goodale, through their various disciplines and areas of expertise, have
helped me better understand and appreciate the vitality of history and the
subjectivity of its interpretation.

My newfound knowledge of shipbuilding also owes a great deal
to the efforts of the late
John Patrick Sarsfield and a ship he saw finished only in his mind.
His replica of the caravel *Niña*, built for the Columbus Foundation of St. Thomas, U.S.
Virgin Islands, which I was fortunate enough to see both under construction in Brazil
and fully rigged in Rhode Island, is undoubtedly the most accurate and authentic
vessel of its kind afloat.

I wish to thank
Robert McNulty, of Partners for Livable Places in Washington, D.C., who planted
the seed for this project in 1985 with his infectious
enthusiasm for underwater archaeology, and
Jan Adkins, author, illustrator, and colleague at Rhode Island School of Design, to
whose wisdom, among other things, is owed the fact that this book mercifully
stops at ninety-six pages.

Library of Congress Cataloging-in-Publication Data

Macaulay, David.
  Ship / David Macaulay.
    p. cm.
  Summary: Describes wooden ships or caravels of the fifteenth
century and follows archaeologists as they uncover a lost caravel in
the Caribbean Sea.
  ISBN 0-395-52439-3
  1. Caravels—History—Juvenile literature.   2. Caravels—Caribbean
Area—History—Juvenile literature.   3. Underwater archaeology—
Caribbean Sea—Juvenile literature.   4. Shipwrecks—Caribbean Sea—
Juvenile literature.   5. Caribbean Sea—Antiquities—Juvenile
literature.   [1. Caravels—History.   2. Ships—History.
3. Underwater archaeology.   4. Shipwrecks.   5. Caribbean Sea—
Antiquities.]   I. Title.
VM311.C27M33   1993   92-1346
387.2'1—dc20   CIP
                             AC

Printed in the United States of America

HOR   10   9   8   7   6   5   4   3   2   1